The Oyster Garden

A NOVEL

Kristin Kraus

QUEEN BEE PRESS

Calgary

Copyright c 2009 Kristin Kraus All rights reserved.

The use of any part of this publication reproduced, transmitted in any form or by any means, electronic, mechanical, photocopying, recording, or otherwise, or stored in a retrieval system, without prior written consent of the publisher is an infringement of copyright law.

This is a work of fiction. Names, characters, places, and incidents are either a product of the author's imagination or are used fictitiously. Any resemblance to actual persons, living or dead, events or locales is entirely coincidental.

Library and Archives Canada Cataloguing in Publication

Kraus, Kristin, 1966-
      The oyster garden / Kristin Kraus.

ISBN 978-0-9808896-1-1

      I. Title.

PS8621.R38O98 2009   C813'.6   C2009-902196-X

Queen Bee Press
40 Strathridge Gardens SW
Calgary, Alberta T3H 3S1
www.queenbeepress.org

Printed in Canada

For Blair

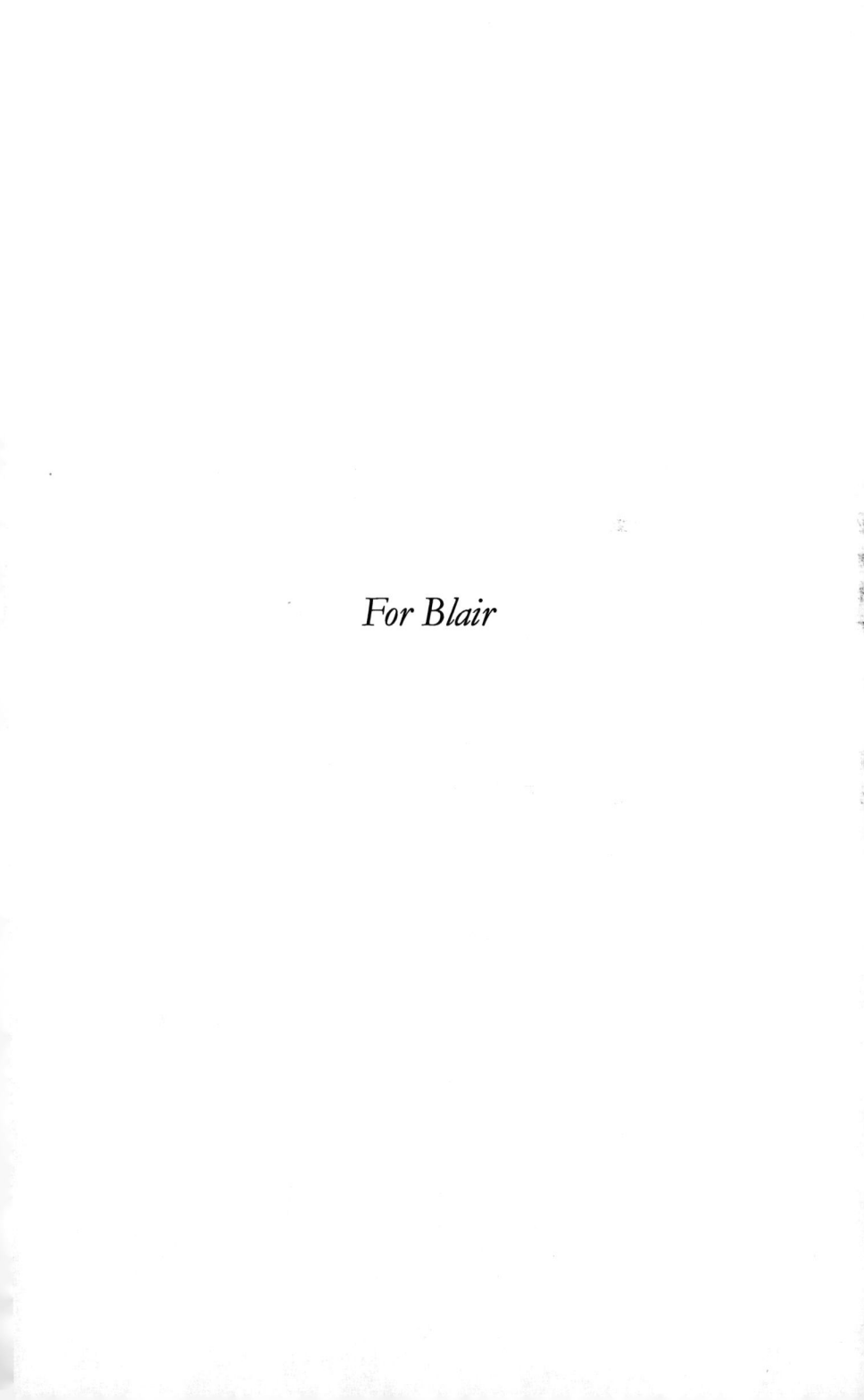

Acknowledgements

As solitary a pursuit as writing is, no book is published without help from others. I thank with all of my heart Gayl Veinotte, Pat Kozak, Marie Babcock, Laurie Campbell, Dana Longeway and Heather Pfeiffer. Their professionalism is much appreciated.

Also by Kristin Kraus

Monkey Sandwich Stories

CHAPTER 1

Cape Charles, Virginia
October

The front screen door slammed, and Harriet stormed into the kitchen, bringing with her a cyclone of after-school trappings. Maggie sighed, recognizing the end of her quiet time. Her teen was home: let the drama begin. Lifting herself out of the deck chair, she closed the journal she'd been writing in and drained the last sip from a glass of cold white wine. Inside, she greeted her fourteen-year-old in the kitchen, noting that Harriet had tossed her knapsack on the nearby couch. Maggie winced — all the dirty floors that knapsack had been dragged along, a myriad of germs and filth picked up from a school full of pimply teenagers tainting her off-white couch.

"Keep the bag on the floor, Hanky," Maggie said, moving the offending item to the tile floor. Her daughter's given name was Harriet, but as a toddler, she had bull-dozed everything and everybody, so her husband, Silas, had nicknamed her "Hank the Tank." He shortened it to "Hanky," and the nickname had remained in use, at home at least.

"What did you do at school today?" Maggie asked. She popped a fresh piece of spearmint gum into her mouth, hoping to cover her stale wine breath.

Harriet grunted. "Not much," she said. She threw open the fridge door, as if to surprise someone inside. Not satisfied with groceries enough to feed a small village, she pulled open the freezer door, grabbed two frozen waffles and popped them into the toaster. Maggie pressed her lips together and refrained from asking if Harriet had washed her hands. Having been told before that she was a relentless nag, she resolutely pushed away thoughts of bacteria and necrotizing fasciitis.

Maggie poured herself tea as Harriet downed a tall glass of chocolate milk. Belching, she poured a second glass, half full this time. "Excuse me," she said with an impish smile.

"Close your mouth when you burp."

"I said excuse me," Harriet answered, as if those two simple words made up for any egregious behaviour. Just then, the toaster waffles jumped, and, with a practised flourish, Harriet lifted the hot circles out of the toaster with index finger and thumb, flinging them onto a small plate. She mushed blobs of butter onto the steaming waffles, effectively flattening them. Golden streams of sweet syrup followed. Still standing at the counter, she attacked the hot snack with knife and fork, shovelling large pieces of waffle into her mouth.

"What kind of homework do you have today?" Maggie asked.

"Science project." The girl swallowed a formidable chunk. Maggie watched her add more syrup to the waffles and bit her tongue. At Harriet's age, she'd only had the fake maple syrup and they weren't allowed to put so much on. After all, as her father had been fond of saying, money doesn't grow on trees. Maggie had always wanted to retort that maple syrup did, but knew better.

"Gotta start and maintain an oyster garden." Harriet licked a bit of syrup from her finger and tucked a stray piece of blond hair behind her ear.

Maggie knew all about oysters and other marine life from her biology classes; she had a bachelor of science. She had grown up in Richmond, Virginia, and had lived in the marine environment of Cape Charles since she and Silas had married.

"What kind of equipment do you need for that?"

Harriet finished her last bite, wiped her hands on her jeans and went over to the couch. She hesitated there a moment, trying to place her knapsack, then realized her mother had moved it. She dug around inside and pulled out some crumpled papers.

Straightening them out, she read aloud in a voice that mimicked her science teacher, "You need either wire mesh boxes or a rectangular frame." In her own voice, she added, "We don't have anything like that."

"We can go to the hardware store."

"Aw, man," her daughter moaned, "do we hafta build stuff? That's so lame."

"Actually, it's kind of fun, sort of like doing a jigsaw puzzle." As soon as she spoke, Maggie knew she wasn't convincing her daughter of anything.

"Puzzles bite." Harriet slumped her shoulders and groaned.

The beginnings of a tension headache played at Maggie's temples; she longed for the days when Harriet was younger and easier to get along with. Plugging on optimistically, she offered to help.

"Do you want to build the Taylor float or the oyster cage?" she asked, to which the girl shrugged and picked something out from beneath her fingernail. Maggie passed her a sheet of paper. "Read me the advantages and disadvantages of each."

Harriet read in a monotone. When she finished, Maggie asked which would work better on their docks.

"The oyster cages," Harriet said. Maggie pressed her for more information. "Oyster cages are easier to clean than Taylor floats; they're not as heavy to lift out of the water."

Maggie was delighted to find her daughter must have paid some attention in class; she had sound reasons for her choice.

"Now Harriet, the cleaning of these cages is your responsibility—"

"I know, I know." Her daughter cut her off, rolling her eyes. "Can I do this later, Mom? I'm bagged." Not even waiting for an answer, she went off to find solace in the TV. Maggie used her cold tea to swallow two tablets for her now full-blown headache.

Maggie washed her face and liberally applied that magic talisman, anti-wrinkle cream. Her husband, Silas, had come home from work late and was reading the newspaper in bed. Maggie told him how she and Harriet had bought materials for building the oyster cages after supper that evening. Silas continued to the business section. When her voice trailed off mid-sentence, he didn't notice.

In flannel pyjamas, Maggie got under the covers and turned her back to him. Silas put down his newspaper and reached over to touch her upper arm; Maggie recoiled.

"I'm really tired and I have a headache," she said over her shoulder. Rebuffed, Silas shrugged, picked up his newspaper and continued to read the business section.

The next evening, Maggie approached Harriet's bedroom to tell her to come down to the kitchen for supper. Through the bedroom door, Maggie could hear her daughter talking on the phone. She listened and heard Harriet say that her mother used to be really pretty, but had let herself go. Worse than that, she said her mom didn't do anything all day long. Slinking away, Maggie retreated to her own bedroom. She locked the door and cried into her pillow.

She could only allow herself a few minutes of overt sadness. Forcing herself off the bed, she padded into the bathroom to stare into the mirror. She rinsed her face in cold water and patted it dry. Her eyes, bloodshot from crying, stared back. She reached for the eye-drops and gave each a generous dose. In the full-length mirror, she examined her figure from the front and sides. She saw a tall, solidly built woman in dowdy clothes. She went to the closet and pulled all her clothes off their hangers and tossed them in a pile on the floor, deciding that her next project was to go through them and keep only the ones that were stylish, just like the reality shows on TV. She blew her nose one last time and returned to Harriet's bedroom door. In as cheerful a voice as she could muster, she announced that dinner was ready. Downstairs, she warmed the cold food, plate by plate, in the microwave.

Before Harriet left for school the following morning, she peeked inside her lunch bag to see what Maggie had packed for her.

"Puke! Mom, you know I don't like turkey sandwiches!" She took the offending item from her bag and held it aloft, as one might a dead rat.

"So, tell me what you like. Don't just complain about what you don't." She struggled to keep her voice even. Silas came into the kitchen and poured himself a cup of coffee.

"What's going on?" he asked, taking a sip.

"Harriet is telling me what she thinks of the lunch I packed for her." Maggie answered, feeling like a tattletale.

"And I don't like yoghurt. It's hard to open and then it

gets all over everything. Ick." She set the unopened container on the counter.

"Well, it seems to me that you're old enough to be making your own lunch, Hanky," Silas said, an edge to his voice. Turning on Maggie, he added, "Why do you still make her lunch? Clearly, she doesn't appreciate it." Maggie had no answer.

Harriet shrugged, picked up her knapsack and let the screen door slam on her way out. Maggie absentmindedly picked up the yoghurt and turkey sandwich and put them back in the fridge; she would eat them herself for lunch.

When Maggie asked her daughter after school that day if she had finished her science work, Harriet avoided eye contact. "I got some of it done, but I forgot to do the last part of the sheet."

"Hanky! Let me see what you have so far." Maggie put out her hand imperiously, and after some rummaging in her bag, the girl produced a crumpled paper with scant writing on it.

Maggie's eyes widened. "You've barely started it!"

"I'll do the rest tonight," Harriet said, turning away with a roll of her eyes.

"You certainly will!" Maggie heard her own voice, shrill and loud. "You won't talk on the phone or go anywhere until it's done properly!"

"Mom," Harriet whined, but Maggie cut her off.

"Don't go there, Harriet! This is shoddy work! Absolutely unacceptable!"

Harriet grabbed the paper from her mother and shoved it back in the bag. "It'll be good enough, Mom," she muttered.

"You need to change your attitude, young lady! You're just being lazy." Maggie flushed hotly.

"Mom, you're calling me names." Harriet's voice quavered and she started to cry. Maggie knew that she should stop talking, but something in her opened up like a burst dam.

"I am not calling you names!" she shouted, digging the hole yet deeper. "Now get upstairs and finish your homework!" Her voice faltered; she felt that familiar trembling in her gut.

"But, Mom!" Harriet protested, standing at the base of the stairs. Then she screamed, "I don't even care about my marks!"

"You should! That work is crap!" Maggie shrieked.

Harriet stood, defiant, refusing to move.

"Get upstairs!" Maggie yelled, rage overtaking her. Harriet tried to argue some more, but Maggie chased her up the stairs, not sure what she would do if she caught her. Harriet ran into her bedroom, slamming the door in Maggie's face. Maggie stopped outside her daughter's bedroom door, chest heaving from the exertion, and pounded her fists on the closed door. Both mother and daughter were crying by now.

Harriet shouted, "I hate you!"

"I hate you, too," Maggie screamed back at her. She thumped down the hall to her own bedroom, where she ground mascara and tears into her pillow case.

Silas trotted upstairs after work to change out of his suit and into sweats and a T-shirt. Maggie followed him up, a glass of red wine in her hand. She held it carefully, mindful of the white carpet.

"I lost my temper again with Harriet," she told him as she watched him hang up his pants.

"Yeah?" he worked his tie loose and reached for the rack to hang it up. "She's been a little difficult lately, hey?"

"I really did it this time," she said, looking down at her hands, as if the answers were written there. Silas seemed distracted, smoothing the tie on its hanger.

"I told her, her school work was crap." Maggie lowered her head. "And that I hated her." She whispered this last part.

Silas slid the tie-rack back into place and stared at her, hearing her for the first time. "Oh, Maggie," he said.

"I didn't mean it; I was just angry." Maggie's words tumbled out and she put down her glass. Her voice strained as she said, "She can be so trying sometimes."

Silas shook his head and pulled her towards him in a long embrace. "She can be a real Hanky sometimes."

"I thought you were going to yell at me," Maggie sniffled. He shook her head and held her for a long time.

By bedtime, Maggie was ready to apologize; she found her daughter in her bedroom reading. Harriet put her science-fiction novel face-down on the bedcovers.

"Sweetheart, I am so sorry for what I said to you earlier." Maggie approached gingerly, not sure of the reception she would get, and patted Harriet's shoulder.

"It's okay, Mom." Tears sprang to Maggie's eyes and she hugged her daughter tightly.

"No, honey, it's not. You didn't deserve that, me shouting at you. I'm sorry." She squeezed her eyes shut as tears fell on Harriet's shoulders. How is it that we go from being everything in the eyes of our children to being so fallible as they grow? Harriet pulled back from the hug and looked into her mother's red eyes.

"Is it hard being a mom?" she asked.

"Sometimes, because when your kids are little you have to do everything for them and make all the decisions. As they get older, they don't need you to do that, but by then, it's become a habit for the mom. I guess I need to realize that you can make some of your own decisions, now. It's hard is for me sometimes, though. I love being your mom and I love you." Maggie clasped her daughter again, burying her face in Harriet's long blond hair. It smelled of fresh shampoo. Pulling away gently after a few minutes, Maggie said, "I overheard you talking on the phone about me the other day."

Harriet's face fell. Her eyes darted left and right. She smiled weakly and raised her eyebrows.

"I heard my name and couldn't help but listen," Maggie continued. "Maybe you think I don't do much all day, but I do run the household, and that takes time and energy." Harriet tried to interrupt, but Maggie put her hand up. "Let me finish, Hanky. I feel fortunate that your father earns enough that I can stay at home. It allows me to be more present for the two of you and also to have time to take care of myself." Maggie felt a stab of guilt; she had not really been properly taking care of any of them, least of all herself. Merely reading about self-care in magazines was not the same as actually doing it.

"Sorry, Mom," Harriet said quietly, head down.

"It's all right, dear. I'm sorry I yelled at you and chased you. I won't do it again." Maggie knew she had to keep that promise; she couldn't keep blowing up at Harriet and pleading loss of self-control. Too much was at stake.

Maggie awoke to the sound of birds twittering outside. The pleasant morning song was immediately sullied by the memory of her fight with Harriet. The anger that crackled between them made Maggie want to put the pillow over her head, roll over and go back to sleep forever. Instead, she got up, opened her window blinds for some natural light and then returned to bed with her journal and a pen, her pillows arranged behind her back; she wrote for a long time.

When she finally put the pen down, she knew she'd have

to get up for real. She stepped over the unruly pile of rejected clothes, left where she had tossed them. Almost everything she owned was crumpled on the floor; she had to choose something from there or go naked. Drinking her coffee at the kitchen table, she watched Harriet make her own lunch and resisted the urge to pipe up with suggestions for proteins, carbohydrates and snacks. For a change, the morning passed without a showdown between mother and daughter. Feeling good about that small victory, Maggie phoned her friend.

"Hi, Wendy! How are you feeling?" Maggie knew Wendy suffered from a bit of morning sickness.

"Oh, much better, thanks!" her friend answered. Maggie could hear wailing in the background. "I'd be perfect if I didn't also have to chase a two-year-old around the house feeling like a cow!" They chatted a bit about mundane subjects and then Wendy asked, "Are you all right, Maggie? You seem a bit blue."

It gave her permission to admit to the real reason she'd picked up the phone.

"You know, I had post-partum depression after Genevieve was born, but I found a really good therapist," Wendy said. "I mean, I realize you don't have post-partum. Harriet's a teenager, for God's sake!" she laughed.

"You? Depressed?" Maggie said. "You always seem so together."

Wendy laughed, "Seem is the operative word. I was a wreck and seeing this lady really helped me."

Depression was a concept Maggie associated with the Great Depression; it also made her think of misfits, people who were weak of character, not strong enough mentally or emotionally to handle daily life. Surely, this wasn't her? Yes, she could roust herself from the fetal position, make supper, drive places, but her feelings of inadequacy and anger made her feel like a failure. Was that what depression was? Maggie had no desire to go to therapy, but she had little to lose at this point but her pride. Maybe this lady could help her with Harriet. And Silas. She took down the therapist's phone number and booked herself an appointment.

The drive to the psychologist's office was nerve wracking. Embarrassed to need the help, Maggie worried that she would see someone she knew. Still, she reasoned, if they were there, then they were seeing a therapist, too.

Filling out the forms the psychologist gave her, she stopped, puzzled at question four: "Why have you come for treatment?" There was space for only a short answer. Maggie chewed her lip, wondering how to answer such a complex question on such a short line. The psychologist had left her alone to complete the task in the waiting room. Finally, she scribbled: anger, anxiety, nightmares.

The office door opened, and Lida Matthews welcomed her inside. Maggie sat down in one of two rather comfy looking chairs, and Lida chose the chair directly across from her.

"So, you're angry," Lida began, crossing her legs. "What do you do?"

Maggie knit her brow at the question. She didn't think Lida was asking about jobs or her current status as a stay-at-home mom because she had Maggie's forms in her lap. "What do you mean?" she asked.

"I mean, do you drink? Smoke like a chimney? I can see that you aren't over-eating. Do you do drugs, prescription or street? Gamble compulsively? Binge and purge?" Lida allowed her voice to trail off.

"I guess I 'do' liquor." Maggie answered cautiously. "I mean, I'm not an alcoholic, but I do like beer and wine. A lot."

Lida nodded. "And tell me more about what brings you here today." She jotted down a few notes.

"Well, I've been irritable with my husband and daughter. I mean, my anger is really over the top and I can't seem to control my outbursts." Maggie told Lida about the incident with Harriet.

Lida wrote down something else. "If anger isn't dealt with in a healthy manner, it comes out elsewhere in our lives. Why are you so angry, or with whom are you angry?"

"My husband, my upbringing," Maggie answered immediately. "I know it's a cliché to blame parents for everything, but I really am angry at them. Not just for things that happened when they were raising me, but for things they still do that drive me crazy."

"Was there abuse or neglect?" Lida asked softly.

Maggie shook her head. "No, we had everything we needed materially, but not emotionally. Feelings didn't matter in our house, not the negative ones, anyway. No one wanted to hear it."

"Actually, what you describe is a type of neglect. It's typical of many families of your vintage. All the same, I know it hurts. Tell me more about your relationship with your husband."

While Maggie unloaded to Lida Matthews, Harriet let herself into the house. School had ended early for teacher meetings, so she turned on the TV to watch some of her favourite shows she had taped. After a few hours, she decided to paint her toenails and wandered up to her parents' bathroom to find polish and a nail file in her mother's cabinets. Rifling through various bottles of lotions and trinkets, she noticed false eyelashes that she had never seen her mother wear, lipstick that was too red and various rejected eye shadows, almost new. She waited for her freshly painted toenails to dry and flopped onto her mother's side of the bed. She opened the drawer of the night table beside it, curious to see what her mother kept there. On top of various water colour paintings and crafts that Harriet must have done when she was a child, was her mother's journal. Harriet closed the drawer, and then opened it again. Temptation got the better of her and she lifted out the journal and opened it to somewhere in the middle. She read:

> *Here I sit, broken-hearted. Ah, the forties. It used to be called middle age. That was before modern medical practices allowed us to live far beyond the point where we'd even want to. I've been doing a lot of thinking lately; hitting rock bottom will do that to you. In my twenties, I thought I had left my crappy upbringing behind. In my thirties, I was naively waiting for life to get better. Now, I realize that my life is what I have signed up for. Not always a pretty thought. So I have a choice: deal with the demons of the past, or continue to ignore them. Dealing is harder in the short term, but ignoring them is worse in the long run. I'm going to improve my lot in life, dammit, or twist myself into a pretzel trying.*

At the sound of the garage door opening, Harriet slammed the journal closed and quickly placed it back where she found it. She ran down to greet her mother — something she rarely did.

"To what do I owe this pleasure?" Maggie asked, bearing the brunt of an exuberant hug. "Why are you looking at me like that?" she asked her daughter. Harriet stared at her for a minute and then kissed her on the cheek.

"No reason, Mom. Love you." Harriet picked her bag off the floor and settled down at the table to do some homework. Maggie shook her head, bewildered, but glad for the affection, however rare these days.

Harriet listened to her music up in her bedroom and wondered about what she had read. Was her mother really so unhappy? Was it Harriet's fault?

As for Silas, he'd grown up in a generation that believed therapists were the preserve of rock stars and basket cases (not mutually exclusive). He was shocked when Maggie told him she had been to see one. But Lida had suggested that the couple spend a week away, just the two of them, to reconnect and reaffirm their marriage. Silas liked the idea, so Maggie looked into flights and hotels and arranged for Beryl, Silas's mother, to come and stay with Harriet.

Maggie dropped Harriet and her friend off at the recreation centre; they wanted to go swimming. As she put her hands to the steering wheel to pull away from the curb, she glanced at her left hand and gasped. Her wedding ring was still on her left finger, but the diamond was gone, the tall claws holding nothing, the setting remarkably ugly without its stone. Slamming the vehicle into park, Maggie searched frantically around the front seat and outside pavement for the lost diamond. A woman in a black SUV honked. Maggie knew that she was in a drop-off zone and should move, but didn't care. She gave the woman the finger, mouthing the words to go with it and continued her search. At the reception desk of the pool, she left her name and number in case someone should return it, knowing, however, that it would be unlikely.

At home, she searched the vacuum canister, the garage and her floors. She didn't know exactly when or where it had fallen out. The ring was likely still intact that morning, but she couldn't say for sure. What would Silas say? He had bought her that ring when they had married at age 21, spending more than three months' salary, more than they could afford at that age. The diamond had been on the small side, but of good quality. She sat at the kitchen table with a cup of tea and took the empty gold band off her finger. The bare claws were covered with a grey sludge, the detritus of years of living, but nothing a little jewellery cleaner couldn't solve. Maggie tucked the shell of a ring into a little-used kitchen cupboard and left the house again to pick up Harriet and her friend.

CHAPTER 2

"If nothing changes, nothing changes." — *Anonymous*

It was a Sunday in November when Silas and Harriet went outside in the back yard to set up the oyster garden for Harriet's project. Maggie watched them out the window as she made sandwiches for lunch; Harriet was lying on her back on the grass while Silas wiped his brow with a cloth and squinted as he wrestled with rope and wire mesh cages. She went to the door and called Harriet in to set the table. She had to call three times before Silas admonished the girl to respond.

"I'm busy," Harriet whined.

"No, you're not. I'm doing everything so far," Silas answered. "In you go."

After lunch, all three of them went to the Chesapeake Bay Hatchery to pick up their oysters. Inside, they approached the front desk; a woman wearing large amethyst earrings and a ponytail greeted them. Her name tag said "Prudence."

"We're here for oysters for a garden," Maggie told her, feeling immediately that she should let Harriet do the talking; it was her project, after all. So hard not to take over everything, she thought. Harriet lugged inside a large blue plastic tub Silas had brought, and Prudence led them out the back door of the building towards several docks. She told Silas to fill the tub half full of sea water as Prudence lifted a few cages out of the water and onto the dock. The baby oysters — spat — were stuck together. They all helped to scoop the cultch, oysters with babies attached, into small pails and then into the tub. Prudence said the oysters needed a good start before being planted in sanctuary reefs, once well established. Harriet would fill out data sheets monthly and email them to the hatchery.

A week later, Maggie was back in Lida Matthews's office. Lida gestured to the nearby coffee pot for Maggie to help herself as she settled into her usual chair.

"How is it going on that medication, Maggie?" Matthew had an arrangement with the GP down the hall. If she felt someone could benefit from a light pharmaceutical, he wrote the prescription.

"It's better. I feel more on an even keel, less like crying at the drop of a hat. No side effects, either. And I haven't had any night-time panic attacks since I've been on it."

"Well, that's good news. And how's Silas with all of this?"

Maggie smiled sheepishly. "Well, I didn't actually tell him about the medication. He's the kind of person who thinks that only hypochondriacs take pills. I don't want him to think

I've gone all Desperate Housewives on him. It's taking him a while to get used to the idea that his wife needs to see a therapist."

Lida frowned a little. "There's no shame in taking medication or talking to someone when you need to, you know, Maggie."

As for Harriet, Maggie felt that her apology had been accepted and mentioned to Lida that the oyster project seemed to give both Maggie and Silas a positive way to help Harriet and encourage her learning. Opening her purse, Maggie unwrapped a square of tissue paper and passed her empty ring to Lida for examination. "The diamond fell out somewhere. I searched for it and ended up giving some poor lady the finger." She smiled a little at this last confession. She added in a quiet voice, "I haven't told Silas that I've lost it. We've already made a few claims on our insurance."

"Isn't that what insurance is for?" Maggie looked down at the hands in her lap and a few tears splashed on her hands. She wrapped the ring and tucked it into the change pocket of her wallet.

"It seems like our marriage is drifting. Losing the diamond feels like a symbol of the love we've lost. I know it sounds childish, but I keep thinking he's going to be mad at me, even though it's not my fault."

"Do you often think things are your fault when they aren't?"

Maggie nodded. "Yes, and it makes me feel lousy. I feel

like I grew up with a lot of responsibility, but none of the privileges that go along with it. I'm angry because it wasn't fair; I was just a kid, but they expected me to function as a parent because they were half in-the-bag. I look at my life now and think I should feel grateful because I have so much — a husband, daughter, lovely home, more than enough money. Why am I so unhappy?" Maggie pulled a Kleenex out of its nearby box and blew her nose.

"It's natural to be angry about the injustices in your life. You wouldn't be honest with yourself if you didn't acknowledge those feelings, but it's time to let go of that anger because it isn't serving you well." Matthews paused and then changed the subject. "How's your sex life with Silas?" she asked, jotting something down in her notebook.

"We probably have sex two or three times a week, missionary style. You know, it's not bad, considering."

Lida raised her eyebrows, "Wow, I'm surprised you have sex with him at all, you're so angry with him."

"Every magazine article on the topic says that when your sex life disappears, that's the end of the marriage. I don't want to give him a reason to have an affair." Maggie crumpled up her Kleenex and tossed it in the nearby garbage can.

"Do you think he would, or has?" Maggie thought not. Lowering her voice slightly, Lida asked, "Do you have suicidal thoughts?"

"Sometimes, when I drive into the garage, I think it would be so easy to just pull down the garage door and let the vehicle run."

"I appreciate your honesty," Lida said, nodding and writing in her book. "How seriously do you consider this?"

"I'd never do it. I know how awful it would be for my family."

"Yes, it would. I think your problems are solvable, though, Maggie. Sounds to me like you and Silas have some work to do on your marriage, but it seems to have a strong foundation. Some counselling would help the two of you to strengthen your marriage. And when couples 'get right' with each other, problems with children tend to subside. It might take some time and patience, but it will come. "

Maggie left the office feeling much lighter. She had a cup of tea with Wendy before Harriet came home from school.

Kristin Kraus

CHAPTER 3

"Can't get no serenity." — Anonymous

Maggie woke early from a fitful sleep; her heart still pounded from her nightmare. She'd dreamed that she'd checked on the oysters and they were all dead and rotting. She was terrified by Harriet's anger and cried in her sleep. She lifted herself out of bed slowly and peered between her curtains at the morning sky. The sun wasn't up yet, but the stars were fading. Slipping on jeans and a fleece jacket, she nipped outside and onto the dock where the water lapped gently against its wood. The cool air fresh on her face filled her with hope. Harriet's oyster cages bobbed just under the water's surface. Silas and Harriet had made four cages, guessing that more cages with fewer oysters in them would be lighter to lift out of the water for cleaning. There was an autumn chill in the air, and Maggie shivered as she lifted one of the cages up and shook it. Oysters bounced around inside; she remembered reading that oyster shells can grow into the mesh cage if they are not moved frequently. She wondered if Harriet knew that.

Grandma Beryl arrived on a Friday evening. She shuffled in the door with her compact hard-sided burgundy suitcase. Before she even took off her coat, she opened the suitcase to give Harriet a gift. Harriet beamed and held up to her body a brand-new pair of silky blue pyjamas.

"Thank you, Gram!" Harriet grabbed Beryl in a big hug, and Maggie could see that Harriet was a good foot taller than her grandmother, maybe more than a foot; Beryl's hair, like a dandelion gone to seed, puffed up about two inches.

As Silas poured his mother a cup of strong tea, Maggie went over the various contact phone numbers with her and the schedule of Harriet's activities.

"Oh, yes, and there's Harriet's oyster garden."

Beryl silenced Maggie with a raised hand. "That will be Hanky's department. I don't do oysters," she said bluntly.

"Did you hear that, Harriet?" Silas said, "It's all up to you." Harriet nodded, pouting slightly.

"They'll be in good hands," Beryl said, patting Harriet on the shoulder. Once the parents had left for their trip, Beryl and Harriet made popcorn and milkshakes. Beryl found the movie "Breakfast at Tiffany's" on one of the TV channels, and Harriet watched it with her, enjoying it even though it wasn't the kind of movie she normally would have chosen.

The next day, Beryl reminded Harriet to check the oyster garden. Harriet came tearing into the house, bawling.

"What is it?" Beryl asked, putting her arm around the lanky girl.

"Come, look!" Harriet yelled, pulling Beryl by the arm out to the dock. She pointed to one of the oyster cages that had broken completely away from its moorings. Looking hard, Beryl could see it lodged at the bottom of the bay near the dock.

"It's not supposed to be like that! It has to be suspended!" Harriet shrieked. Beryl was quiet for a moment.

"So, what will you do?" she finally asked.

"I don't know!" Harriet wailed. Beryl breathed in deeply; patience wasn't her strong suit.

"What can you do?"

"Well, duh. Go get it, but how?" Harriet started to cry.

"Well, can you swim?" she asked, knowing full well that Harriet could.

"Yes, but the water's cold this time of year." Harriet wiped tears from her cheeks.

"And, what do people around here wear in the water when it's cold?" Beryl prompted.

"A wet suit!" Harriet exclaimed. "And we have one!" Her face lit up and she raced to the shed to get it.

"My work here is done," Beryl said to herself as she walked back to the house. She watched out the kitchen window as Harriet dove into the bay in her wet suit and brought the oyster cage up from the bottom. She attached it temporarily to the dock with a bungee cord. Beryl got a towel from the linen closet for Harriet's return.

Dripping on the floor in the entrance of the house, Harriet beamed.

"This was the problem." She held up a broken piece of rope. "It must have rubbed against the dock until it frayed completely." She dropped the piece of rope and caught the towel Beryl tossed her way. She dried off and took off her wet suit.

"How can you fix that?"

Harriet was so quiet, her grandmother thought the girl had not heard her. Just as she was about to repeat the question, Harriet burst out, "I have a few website addresses that Prudence gave me!" and tore off to the computer to find out what to do next. Beryl neither knew nor cared who Prudence was. She shuffled off to the kitchen for more tea.

About ten minutes later, Harriet stormed out of the den. "Gram," she shouted as she put on her coat, "can you drive me to the hardware store?"

"What do you need from the hardware store?"

"Garden hose. Isn't that brilliant? You put your rope inside a garden hose to keep it from chafing and breaking!" Harriet gestured impatiently at Beryl. "Let's go!"

"Can I finish my tea?" Beryl looked longingly into the teacup she was still cradling in her hands.

"Bring it along!" Harriet said, setting a travel mug down in front of her.

"You're such a little turd!" Beryl laughed, pouring her tea into the travel mug, and off they went.

The Oyster Garden

Over hamburgers in the kitchen afterwards, Beryl said she couldn't believe how much money they had just spent on garden hose for the project. "Isn't there a better use for that money?" she asked Harriet.

Harriet rolled her eyes. "Grandma, the Chesapeake Bay oyster is an important species in our ecosystem. We need to preserve it."

"Why?" Beryl asked stubbornly.

Harriet sighed, as if talking to a child, "Because oysters in the wild live in oyster reefs which provide fifty times the surface area of an equally flat bottom, and oyster reefs are home to all kinds of other sea life."

"And what do you do with the oysters when you're done your project?" Beryl asked, interested in spite of herself.

"Plant them in sanctuary reefs. It's a restoration project." Harriet said, chomping down on her burger.

"Glad to see they're teaching you something at school." Beryl chuckled, shaking her head. "Save the oysters!"

Harriet finished her milk and took off outside to refit the ropes and hoses on all four cages. She was out there until dark, so Beryl made sure there was a nice cup of cocoa waiting for her when she returned.

Knowing that her grandmother had gone to bed, Harriet finished her hot chocolate and sneaked upstairs to her mother's bedroom night table where she found Maggie's journal. She justified her snooping by telling herself that she hadn't peeked at it for a while now, and she was curious about what was going on with her mom, knowing she wasn't happy, but not understanding why.

> *Session with Lida went well today. She thinks I am clinically depressed and recommended that I continue to write in my journal to help clarify my feelings. Also, am supposed to try yoga or some other mind-body-spirit thing. Oh yeah, supposed to say my prayers, too. I haven't been a very good Catholic, not a regular church-goer, not holding very Christian attitudes (i.e.: giving people the finger).*

Harriet suppressed a giggle at this; frankly, she had a hard time picturing the alleged bird flip.

> *Lida suggests I tell Silas about my lost diamond on our trip, after we've had some quality time together.*

Lost diamond? Harriet wasn't sure what that referred to.

> *We also talked about my parents' alcoholism and how that still affects me. I guess I thought that since I left home, I was free of cleaning up after them and pretending to be invisible during their hangovers. I remember opening the bathroom door one morning and hitting an obstruction. It was my father's head; he had passed out on the floor. Other*

times his boss would phone and I would make excuses for him since he was still unconscious or sleeping. I thought I had moved on completely from this stuff. I was stunned to consider that my current depression is a direct result all these years later of their legacy. You don't escape an alcoholic home so neatly.

Harriet stopped reading, uneasy with this knowledge. She returned the journal and skulked off to bed where she lay awake, thinking. Who was Lida? It's true, she thought, that she found herself avoiding her maternal grandparents once they had a few glasses of wine, because it seemed to make them belligerent, but did that make them alcoholic? Harriet struggled to reconcile the grandparents she knew today with the image of her mother caring for them because of drunkenness. It was too much to deal with right now and she drifted off to sleep.

A few days later, Beryl heard Harriet hollering from the deck.

"What is it, child? Gosh, don't yell!" She dried her hands on a tea towel, tossed it over her shoulder and hustled out to the dock. She found all the oyster cages pulled up onto the dock and Harriet slumped over with her face in her hands.

"God, what's that funky smell?" Beryl covered her nose with her hands.

"My oysters — they're dead! Their shells are all closed, look." Harriet flung her arm out in the direction of the cages and sniffled. Beryl surveyed the sorry collection of shellfish.

"What now, sweetie?" she said softly.

"I don't know!" Harriet wailed, running to the house and disappearing inside. Beryl left all the cages where they were and went back to the house after her. She loaded the dishwasher while Harriet cried in her bedroom.

Later, a red-eyed Harriet helped herself to a bowl of cereal and sat quietly at the kitchen table.

"What now?" Beryl asked again.

"Now, we count them," she said with a sigh. "Normally, you'd count the live and the dead, but I think they're all dead." She added more sugar to her cereal. "I guess I tell Prudence and get some new ones."

"Oh," Beryl said. "I can help you throw away the dead ones."

"No!" Harriet exclaimed, horrified. "No, Grandma! The dead ones provide habitat. We keep them for the whole time." Then she added , "Do you think Prudence will be angry?"

Beryl got up and ruffled Harriet's hair. "No, honey. I doubt you'd be the first volunteer to kill your oysters." She took some money out of an envelope that Maggie had left for the two of them and off they went to the Chesapeake Bay Hatchery.

In Florida, Silas and Maggie returned to their hotel after a round of golf. Maggie golfed with her friends in a Ladies' League in Cape Charles, but it had been a few years since she and Silas had golfed together. The next afternoon, they each enjoyed a massage in the hotel spa. That night at dinner, Silas told Maggie that she looked beautiful. She was glad she'd bought a new outfit for the trip, a burgundy organza cocktail dress, more expensive than she usually allowed herself. He wanted to know how she was doing these days, which she knew meant that he was concerned about her depression. At least they had a name for it now. Before, she just thought she was going crazy, and Silas probably did, too.

He signalled the waiter for another bottle of wine. Maggie remembered when they were young; even then Silas knew a lot about wines, how to pair them with food, how to taste them while the server stood by. It all seemed a bit of a charade and she half-admired him and half-thought he was full of shit. He was so earnest, though.

"Nice wine, hey?" Silas swirled it around in his glass, admiring its legs.

"I'm afraid so," Maggie answered. "I'm a bit afraid of my love for it, in fact."

Silas looked at her quizzically. "Well, you know what my parents are like," she went on.

"Lushes?" He smiled.

"Yes, and I don't want to be like that." Realizing that Maggie was talking seriously, he reached over and touched her hand.

"You don't have to worry; you're not like that," he reassured her.

Maggie shrugged, less certain. Taking a deep breath, she said, "Silas, what would you say to some marriage counselling?"

He rubbed his freshly shaven chin and looked her steadily in the eye. Finally, he answered, "I don't think we need it. I mean, what do you think it's going to accomplish?"

Maggie fought to tame her frustration. "We have issues, Silas, some of them our own personal issues, some of them shared. I know I'm too needy sometimes and you didn't have the greatest upbringing either…."

"My mom did the best she could," Silas interrupted her, running his hand through his still thick hair. He leaned back in his chair, which Maggie took to mean withdrawal.

"Look, Silas, think about it. I'm not looking to ruin the mood of this lovely romantic dinner. I just want us to move forward as individuals and as a couple. I think counselling could help." She could see the waiter hovering nearby, aware that now might not be the time to ask if they needed anything.

Silas stared out the window of the restaurant where it was now too dark to see the waves. You could still hear them if you listened carefully over the track of restaurant muzak. He smiled weakly at Maggie and nodded. "I'll think about it."

On the last day of their trip, Maggie fessed up about the diamond falling out of her ring; he hadn' t even noticed she wasn't wearing it. To give him credit, he was calm about it, not overjoyed about filing an insurance claim, of course, but philosophically noting that these things do happen. She wondered why she had waited so long to tell him. It had been no big deal; their marriage amounted to so much more than a piece of faceted rock. Silas promised to get her either a new diamond, or a whole new ring. At this, Maggie felt secure, that maybe this was part of a new start.

Kristin Kraus

CHAPTER 4

"He who has seen everything empty itself is close to knowing what everything is filled with." — Antonio Porchia

Back in Virginia in her own back yard, Maggie shielded her eyes from the morning light. She nursed a hangover from too much wine the night before. She'd enjoyed their vacation, but was glad to be home. She surveyed the yard, making mental note of any yard work she could manage, alone or with Harriet's help. Even if Silas had been home — he was working this weekend — he wouldn't likely want to put up the Christmas lights, but if she suggested hiring a professional, he balked. Maybe he had that vestigial caveman instinct that meant only he could perform these tasks. Unfortunately, he seldom got around to it, and it drove Maggie nuts. She met Harriet out on the dock, her cages sitting in the sun; the girl had on her black rubber boots and a thick pullover. She sprayed the oyster cages with a hose.

"Hi, Mom! I'm getting rid of the algae, flatworms and poop," she said gleefully. "Do we have a brush or a paint scraper? I think I'm going to need more force than this garden hose can give it." So much for a heartfelt welcome home. Maggie directed her to the shed, marvelling that she had lived to see the day when her little princess was willingly scraping waste matter off anything. When Harriet was finished, Maggie asked if she could touch one of the oysters.

"Sure, if you want to."

Maggie reached down and opened the cage, carefully lifting out one oyster. Its shell was twice as thick again with barnacles.

"Did you know that the glue that barnacles secrete is the strongest glue known to man?" Harriet said, showing off.

"Didn't know that." Maggie turned the oyster over in her hands. "Their shells are so ugly."

"Yeah, hard to believe that these gross things make pearls," Harriet said. Maggie peered inside the shell; no pearl sat there, nothing but a squishy grey lump of flesh.

"I'll keep looking for pearls. Maybe I'll get lucky," she said jokingly. Back in the house, Maggie took a few pain relief pills and then fought her way through a pile of boxes in the attic to look for Christmas lights. It was a mild day, so she brought the step ladder from the garage and called Harriet over to help untangle the strings. Up on the top part of the ladder, she clipped the lights into the hooks she'd put up the year before, as Harriet fed her the length.

"I thought you were afraid of heights," Harriet said. "Dad said he'd put these up." Maggie bit back the urge to say that if she left it to Silas, the lights wouldn't go up until Christmas eve. Instead, she answered, "I can do it." Maggie didn't need any help with the last few lights, so Harriet returned to her cages, moving them back over the dock. A rattle and crash made her release the last cage hurriedly. She ran back to the side of the house where Maggie lay on the grass, moaning, the ladder on its side nearby. As her mom seemed disoriented, Harriet called Beryl, and the two of them helped Maggie into the car. They took her to the hospital; Silas was the last to know.

Hours later, Maggie left the hospital with an air cast on her left foot. In their TV room, she rested the sore leg on the ottoman while a Silas fixed her a glass of eggnog. He made a big show of asking her if she'd like nutmeg or cinnamon sprinkled on it. "I made it without rum, seeing as how you're on meds," he said, presenting the drink as though afraid she might strike him. "I'm glad it's not broken." He made a vague gesture toward her leg.

"Yeah, just ligaments," Maggie said, her voice weary and low.

"Hey, the Christmas lights look great!" Silas started. "I would have put them up. I've just been busy." Maggie said nothing, just pursed her lips and raised a brow.

"What? I would have," Silas protested.

"Every year, it's the same thing." Maggie said. She twisted her glass in her hand, making the eggnog run up the side of the glass, coating it. "I wait for you to put up the outdoor lights, and then by mid-December, I tire of waiting for you to make it a priority so I just do it. You're a procrastinator. Why pretend any different?" She let out a long, slow sigh.

"I am not." Silas blustered, indignant.

"Have you taken my ring to the jewellers to set a new diamond yet?" Maggie shot back. Silas blushed. "I thought not. You want some say as to what kind of ring I get, but then you don't get around to taking it in. You tie my hands." Maggie scowled and turned on the TV with the remote; she was done with this conversation. Silas stood nearby for a moment and then slunk away.

As the drama between Maggie and Silas played out, Harriet sat on her parents' bed with the bedroom door closed. She read her mother's journal, freezing momentarily when she heard Silas's footsteps. Harriet continued to read when she realized that he was not coming her way.

> *Lida warned me about my own drinking today. If my parents are alcoholic, there is a strong chance genetically that I am one, too. The fact that I use it so often to socialize or relax concerns her. Maybe I should cut down on my drinking.*

Hearing a noise, this time upstairs, Harriet slammed the journal shut and rammed it into the open drawer. She pretended to Silas that she was getting shampoo from their bathroom. Later, in that same bedroom, Maggie worked her way awkwardly to her side of the bed and removed the air cast. Silas pulled back the sheets as she eased herself onto the mattress, but she was too annoyed to accept his help graciously.

"Come on, Maggie. Let's talk," he said. "I'll take your ring to the jewellers' tomorrow. We can upgrade your diamond."

"What jewellers?" Maggie snapped. "You have a full day of meetings tomorrow, so how's that going to work?"

Silas looked down at his hands. "I know I do procrastinate sometimes," he began.

Maggie shook her head in frustration, "You promise things before you even think about whether you can follow through. Anyway, I don't know if I even want a diamond."

Silas's jaw dropped. "How could you not?"

Maggie glared at him and said, "The ring you gave me when we got married was a beautiful ring, but I didn't choose it. We were young and you chose it for me and that's fine, but now I'm older and my tastes have changed." He looked so disheartened, Maggie softened her approach. "All I'm saying is that since we're replacing it, I want to pick it this time. I want something different." She reached out and placed her hand over top of Silas's, a small gesture of goodwill. He nodded, chastened.

Harriet helped her mother out of the car and into the church where Harriet took a course to prepare for the Catholic sacrament of confirmation. Part of that prep included going to confession. Maggie wanted to go too; it had been a while for her and she felt she needed all the forgiveness and divine help she could get. As Harriet held her mother's hand walking up the path to the front doors of the parish, she asked, "Mom, what happened to your wedding ring?" Reflexively, Maggie looked down at her bare left hand.

Fingering her ring finger, she said, "The diamond fell out of its setting and I never did find it."

"Are you going to get another ring?"

"I'm not sure." Maggie shrugged. "There's more to a marriage than a ring, you know." Inside the confessional, an elderly priest greeted Maggie, speaking with a thick Polish accent. He sat quietly as she relayed her sins, those of commission and those of omission (which always sound harmless but are actually the tricky ones). In a shaky voice, she spoke of losing patience with her husband and daughter, drinking too much and not being grateful enough for her blessings. Expecting the standard penance of a few "Hail Mary's" and an "Our Father," she was peeved when Father told her that she was a good woman but needed to try harder. She returned to a pew to pray and wait for Harriet to finish with her confession. Bitterly, she thought, "Are you fucking kidding me? How dare that celibate old man judge me? Who is he to say I need to try harder? I'm busting my ass the best way I know how!" Beneath her outrage, Maggie knew this was not her most serene prayer time ever, and she felt guilty about that, too.

Back in the car, Maggie asked Harriet what penance the elderly priest had given her.

"He said I'm a good girl and that I should treat myself to an ice cream. Can we go for one now?"

Maggie bit her lip and kept silent. If anyone deserved a friggin' ice cream, it was Maggie! Not that Maggie wanted priests to handle children with the fire and brimstone judgment of yesteryear, but ice cream? Sheesh. Maggie refused to take Harriet for ice cream. Mother and daughter both sulked on the way home.

Kristin Kraus

CHAPTER 5

"Better a bottle in front of me than a frontal lobotomy." -
Anonymous

At Lida's office, Maggie sipped coffee from a pottery mug. She'd arrived a few minutes early and waited in the reception area as Lida left for a few minutes. She imagined Lida having a mental sorbet in the back room to cleanse the palate between clients.

Maggie told her she had registered herself for a computer course that started in January.

"So, what are you working towards?"

Maggie wanted to re-enter the job market in her previous field of environmental studies and needed to upgrade her skills and resume. Lida beamed and nodded approvingly.

"Sometimes the plan becomes clearer as we go when we just get started," Lida said. "So, would you go back full time or part time?"

"Probably part time," Maggie said. "I miss having something of my own and I still want to be around for Harriet, but she doesn't need me in the same way she did when she was little." Lida agreed it would also be beneficial for Harriet to see her mother in a working role.

"Maybe, she'll take me less for granted when I'm not waiting for her to get home from school so I 'can serve her'," Maggie said.

"Silas, too." Lida added. Maggie admitted that she had not yet told Silas of her work intentions.

"Oh, tell him. He's a big boy." Lida said.

At her appointment, the physiotherapist was pleased with how quickly Maggie's leg was healing. She needed to continue to do the prescribed exercises, but was on the mend. Maggie bought herself a newspaper and a latte and sat down in the coffee shop to read. She perused all the sections of the paper, saving the lifestyles section (her favourite) for last. With Christmas so close, there were articles about alcohol consumption, how not to trash your reputation at the office party, how to alternate alcoholic and non-alcoholic drinks so as not to get too shit-faced before dinner is served and how to know whether you are an alcoholic. Maggie had been seriously wondering about herself, so this last one caught her eye and she read avidly.

The Johns Hopkins 20 questions required total honesty. Maggie drew a deep breath and decided before starting the quiz to answer as honestly as she knew how. That meant that if she wasn't sure of the answer, she'd consider that an affirmative. Also, Maggie wanted to examine her whole drinking life, from the time she was in her teens, not just the last year or so. Finally, she committed herself to taking action, as in quitting drinking for good, should this test prove her to be alcoholic. She took a sip of her latte, wiped a skiff of foam from her upper lip and dug a pen out from the bottom of her purse.

Maggie considered whether she had ever lost time from work due to drinking. When she worked at the department of environmental quality, there were a few days she had called in sick when she was actually hung over, but at the time, she had justified those as "mental health days." As for whether drinking was making her home life unhappy, she was currently seeing a therapist for anger management and depression, as well as feeling the need for marital counselling; so clearly, yes. The questionnaire asked if she ever turned to lower companions or inferior environments when drinking. As a university student, she and her friends would go to the bars with the cheapest happy hours, many of these the haunt of rubby-dubs. These days, Maggie and her well-heeled friends weren't above sucking up second-hand smoke in a sports pub, getting hammered and laughing bawdily at their own jokes.

Maggie looked up from her newspaper to see if anyone was watching her. Realizing that no one would know what she was doing — it could be a cross-word puzzle after all — she relaxed. Back to her article, she wondered if her drinking made her careless of her family's welfare. The knee-jerk reaction was, of course not; she loved her family very much and she was a damn good mother. Then, uncomfortably shifting in her chair, Maggie remembered the words of the parish priest she had so maligned. She needed to try harder, so the answer was, again, yes. With a sigh of relief, Maggie encountered a few questions she could answer no to, such as do you drink in the morning and do you have financial difficulties as a result of drinking? Buoyed up by a few negative responses, she felt encouraged to think that perhaps she was out of the woods. The next few answers, however, shoved her back down. She did feel remorse after drinking, she did use booze to alleviate worry and, worst of all, she had experienced the piece de resistance of the die-hard alkie, the blackout.

It didn't matter that she hadn't blacked out in years. All that mattered was that a few times in her teen years she had drunk enough to forget what had happened. It's horrible to have others tell you who you kissed (everyone), what you said that was so rude (told your ex-boyfriend's girl to fuck off even though there was no hope of you two ever getting together again — so pathetic), or worse, phoning your girlfriend at four in the morning to give you a ride home from the convenience store and being unable to tell her how you got there in the first place. But for the grace of God, Maggie knew those episodes, as humiliating as they were, could have been even worse. Black outs were the kicker. Non-alcoholics don't black out, period.

At the end of the test, Maggie counted four "no" answers out of twenty questions and looked below to calculate her score. It showed that affirmative answers to any three questions meant you were alcoholic. Maggie stared at people as they walked by. They were buying a cup of coffee, going about their day. Today was changing for her, but probably not for them. She envied them.

Now, I have my answer, she thought, looking back at the newspaper. I said that I wanted to know and now I know. She collected her empty latte cup and left the newspaper on the table, open to the page with the Johns Hopkins test. At home, she researched alcoholism on the Internet and located the time and places for Alcoholics Anonymous meetings in Cape Charles. Then she phoned Lida Matthews.

She was still on the computer when Harriet burst into the room. Maggie reduced the screen so Harriet couldn't see what she was researching.

"Mom, look!" In the girl's palm rested a shiny, round object the size of an overgrown pea. Astonished, Maggie poked it gingerly.

"Is it a…?"

"Pearl," Harriet shouted. "Isn't it cool?"

"It's not from one of your oysters, is it?" Maggie asked, doubtful. Harriet shook her head furiously.

"No, Mom. It takes seven to ten years for an oyster to make a pearl. I got this from Prudence." Maggie fingered the pearl carefully between her forefinger and thumb, pulling it under the desk lamp to better examine it, slightly oblong with a colour between pink and purple.

"It's gorgeous," Maggie said simply. She was surprised that tears sprang to her eyes. Harriet's face fell.

"What's the matter, Mom?" She put her arm around her mother's shoulders.

Wiping her eyes, Maggie explained that she just found it touching and placed the pearl back in Harriet's palm. Harriet told her that it wasn't, by any stretch, a perfect pearl, and that the least expensive cultured pearl rivals the quality of the most expensive natural pearl. Maggie stood up and hugged her daughter tightly for several minutes, delighted that Harriet allowed it.

CHAPTER 6

"Happiness does not consist in keeping what we've got but in enjoying it to the full even as it vanishes." — James Geary

Silas and Maggie talked about Harriet's upcoming first date; well, the first that they were aware of, anyway. Silas was nervous about the idea, but Maggie assured him that the details were all worked out and Harriet would be safe. Their daughter would simply be going to a movie with a boy named Jackson. Silas wasn't happy for two reasons: he had not yet met Jackson, and they were seeing the late movie. Jackson's job at the video store ran until nine o'clock, so they couldn't see the earlier show. When Maggie offered them a ride, but Harriet declined, saying that Jackson's older brother was driving them. Silas started to protest, but Harriet assured him she would call if she needed anything. He was mollified, wanting to trust her. Harriet was to come right home after the movie and definitely no later than 11:30.

Silas answered the phone. It was Wendy's husband calling to say their baby boy was born three days ago. Much to Maggie's annoyance, Silas didn't get any information about the baby like length and weight. Maggie stormed off to the grocery store where she bought ingredients for two lasagnas, one for her family and one for Wendy's. Back home, she shredded cheese and cooked up tomato sauce and then phoned Wendy's husband to arrange a time to bring the warm casserole over and to see the baby.

Wendy answered the door, looking rather perky, considering her sleep deprivation. The baby rested nearby in a bassinet, asleep. Wendy took the lasagna pan and Maggie's coat as Maggie approached the baby and gently moved the blanket back from his face.

"He's beautiful," Maggie cooed. "What did you name him?"

"George," Wendy answered, beaming. "He's seven pounds nine ounces, a big boy!" Maggie nodded. An older lady with red hair and thinly plucked eyebrows reached her hand out to introduce herself. Taking her hand, Maggie said, "You must be Wendy's mother."

Wendy put her arm around her mother's shoulders and said, "She's great! She gets George in the night and brings him to my bed so I can breastfeed him. Then she takes him away, burps him, changes him and helps him get back to sleep."

Maggie smiled, remembering how Beryl had done that for her, too. How simple, yet necessary, was her help at that time of adjustment.

Harriet left for the movies with Jackson as planned, but when she hadn't returned by midnight, a worried Silas went looking for her, driving to various movie theatres and trolling the streets of Cape Charles, searching. As he drove around, becoming more frantic with every passing moment, Maggie phoned all of Harriet's friends to see if they knew where she was. Hanging up after another fruitless call, she heard a screeching sound from the driveway. Opening the front door, she ran out to the driveway and saw an old blue Buick idling there. A young man leaned back in the driver's seat, cigarette dangling from the corner of his mouth, hair hanging in his eyes. Not Jackson, Maggie thought; must be the older brother. In the back seat, a blond boy kissed Harriet; it looked like a long, wet one. Maggie swore and muttered, seeing his hand rustling under Harriet's coat. She banged on the window where the two were necking. Startled, they stumbled out of the back seat.

"Harriet," Maggie said sternly.

"Oh, hi," Jackson greeted Maggie as though they had just run into each other in a perfectly ordinary social situation. "Great movie!" He tilted a bit to one side, as though trying to balance on a moving earth below.

Maggie glared at him and stepped forward to support Harriet, who was weaving on the spot. "Sorry we're late." Harriet blasted her mother with yeasty breath.

"We'll talk about it in the morning," Maggie said tersely. As she led Harriet into the house, Harriet took a detour to the shrubs and threw up. Upstairs, Maggie held her daughter's hair back as she vomited again into the toilet. Solemnly, she tucked her little girl into bed, phoned Silas to let him know that Harriet was home and crawled into her own bed. What frightened Maggie was that she really felt like a drink after all this drama. Tears squeezed out the corners of her eyes as she lay on her back; the garage door opened and closed with Silas's arrival home.

They didn't see the whites of Harriet's eyes until noon. Although furious, Maggie knew this situation needed a delicate parental touch, not just full-out anger. She remembered the time when she was 16 years old, coming home late, drunker than a skunk. Her mother had waited up for her (which was unusual) and scolded her as she clumsily washed her face and brushed her teeth before bed. Maggie expected to be richly lectured and grounded the next day, but her mother said nothing. Maggie wasn't even sure that her father ever knew. In a weird way, Maggie'd been disappointed; she was out of control and needed to be stopped. She was, as the song goes, a hazard to herself.

Silas agreed to stay calm while speaking to Harriet about her state the night before. Maggie hadn't told him about the kiss or the hand up the shirt; if she had, there would be no calm.

They waited until Harriet had eaten breakfast and then they all sat in the living room, Silas gripping the arm of his chair.

"We're disappointed that you came home late and drunk," Maggie began. "What happened?" Harriet stared silently at the floor.

"Did you go the movie?" Maggie asked, forcing her voice to sound as reasonable as possible. Silas shifted his body weight restlessly from one side to the other. Harriet nodded.

"But after the movie, we went to a party that his brother knew about."

"That was a mistake, wasn't it?" Maggie said. Harriet nodded sheepishly.

"You were to come home right after the movie and no later than 11:30!" Silas yelled. Maggie shook her head at him to remind him to simmer down.

"He was giving me a ride home after the party," Harriet insisted.

"If he wasn't going to give you a ride after the movie, you were to call me and I'd come and get you," Maggie said. "And obviously there was alcohol at this party." Harriet nodded again, like a sad bobble-headed doll.

"I know that teenagers are curious about alcohol, and maybe we should have had this conversation sooner, but did you know that there is a history of alcoholism in our family on both sides and that it is genetically inherited?"

Harriet looked up quickly. "On Dad's side, too?"

"How did you know there's alcoholism on my side of the family?"

"Grandma Beryl told me," Harriet said hastily. This made even less sense to Maggie, Beryl being Silas's mother and not knowing her family well at all.

"Two of my uncles are classic cases, Harriet," Silas piped up. "We don't want that to happen to you and we need to know at all times where you are and that you are safe."

"You have to come home when we tell you to or we can't trust you," Maggie added. Harriet nodded, thinking the conversation over. "Because of this, you're grounded for the rest of this weekend, all of next week up to and including next Friday." Harriet looked as though she'd been slapped, burst into tears and ran upstairs, slamming her bedroom door behind her. Silas bounced out of his chair as if to chase her, but Maggie stopped him with a gentle hand to the arm.

"Let her be, Silas."

An hour later, Maggie knocked on Harriet's door. The girl opened it with a grunt. Maggie motioned to the bed, asking silently for permission to sit down beside her daughter. Harriet nodded and Maggie gently stroked her hair.

"Harriet, we love you. You're too young to drink, and we don't want to take you to the hospital to get your stomach pumped. Did you know that people die from alcohol poisoning?" Harriet looked surprised, then allowed Maggie to hug her.

"Also, people do dumb things when they are drunk,

things they wouldn't do or allow done to them if they were sober. You need to ask yourself if Jackson is respectful enough of you."

A chastened Harriet hugged her mother hard and whispered, "Thanks, Mom."

Harriet heard her mother's car drive out of the garage on her way to run errands; she knew that her father had gone outside. In her parents' bedroom, she opened the night table drawer quietly, even though she knew that no one was around to hear its sound, and read more of her mother's journal:

> *For such a common disease, you still don't hear people openly talk about alcoholism. Sometimes they'll refer to someone they know who is a raging alcoholic as having a "drinking problem". Somehow that sounds much better than "alcoholism". Liquor is legal and everywhere; we forget that it can be dangerous; in fact, people in alcohol detox often require medical supervision. We talk of drugs and alcohol, as if alcohol isn't a drug, too. I know that prohibition didn't work, and I'm not saying we should try it again, but geez. As a society, we put up with a lot from booze.*
>
> *At one point does one become an alcoholic? Is it upon the first bitter taste of lager, where you don't even like how it tastes, but you like how it makes*

you feel? Or is it already in your genes, waiting for you to allow alcoholism to take over like weeds in a garden? As a kid, I loved candy; as a teenager, I discovered booze and I've been altered ever since. When life hands me lemons, I make Mike's Hard Lemonade, ha ha.

Hearing Silas enter through the back door of the house startled Harriet and she shoved the journal back in its place. She left the bedroom as she had found it, wondering how her mother could joke about something so serious.

CHAPTER 7

"If you haven't pissed yourself yet, it's coming." — Anonymous quote from an AA meeting

Lida asked Maggie whether she had gone to an AA meeting yet.

"Yes, I went one morning last week for the first time. I've been back every day since then just to make sure I stay sober. I felt good about my first meeting going in, but after about ten minutes, I was bawling. After listening to people tell of their experiences with booze, it dawned on me that I am in the right place. I think there was a part of me that wanted to go to AA and find out that I'm not like them, that I'm not alcoholic and I don't have to quit drinking. Well, that wasn't the case."

Lida passed a box of Kleenex over to Maggie, who dabbed at the tears carefully to avoid smudging her make-up. "Did you earn a chip?"

Maggie smiled, "I sure did! I had been sober already for three days when I got there, so they gave me a coin for twenty-four hours of sobriety. The next one I'll get is for a full week." Lida nodded approvingly and she explained to

Maggie how alcohol is processed differently by women than by men. Women have less water in their bodies due to lower body weight, so a woman's brains and organs are exposed to more alcohol before it gets broken down. As for a glass of wine a day for heart health, Lida informed her that the benefits of lowered coronary risk are mainly in women over the age of 55, and similar benefits can be enjoyed by maintaining a healthy diet, exercising, not smoking and by keeping a healthy weight. Over time, women develop alcohol related diseases more quickly than men, mostly affecting the liver, heart and brain. There is also a strong link between heavy drinking and cancer.

"We psychologists have a little joke: We can't stop you from drinking, but we can sure take the fun out of it for you!" Maggie smiled weakly and then told her about Harriet's drunken episode.

"It sounds like you handled it well, Maggie. Does it bring back bad memories of your teenage drinking to see Harriet drunk?"

"Definitely. I don't want her using alcohol like I did to blot out pain." She went on to explain how she had her first drink at age fourteen, heart-broken after a break-up with a boyfriend. It was the beginning of a long, rich, but not always wonderful, relationship with the bottle. She explained that Silas had been supportive of her quitting. He still drinks, but not as much as he did before she quit.

Meanwhile, stepping over a bag of clothes near her parent's bedroom door, Harriet entrenched herself comfortably in the pillows on their bed and read Maggie's journal:

> *I never learned any positive strategies for dealing with emotional pain. When I felt bad in high school, inferior or invisible, I drank. It served the dual purpose of masking the pain and allowing me to think I was sophisticated and funny. Because I only drank on the weekends at parties, I didn't think I had a problem. Looking around me, many of my peers drank, some of them more than I did, and every adult in my life was a drinker; the ones who didn't had a reliance on something else like soft drinks or cigarettes.*
>
> *It got so I actually blacked out a few times, which scared the crap out of me. I knew from school lectures that only alcoholics black out; I had heard of AA, but thought that it was for old people. Surely no seventeen year-olds went to AA? I never went to AA because I denied to myself that I was alcoholic. I vowed to "cut back". Because I was able to temporarily control my drinking (or so I thought), I considered myself all right; little did I know that I had gone down an unforgiving path.*

Harriet worried that perhaps she had turned herself into an alcoholic by getting drunk that Friday night. It had been fun, feeling dizzy, delightfully irresponsible. The next morning had been bad, though. She had never seen her parents so angry.

Later that evening, Maggie moved most of the furniture towards the walls, creating a space in the middle. It looked to Silas that she was dancing slowly without music.

"What are you doing?"

"Tai chi," she answered, arms flowing as if carried on a light breeze. "Each move has a name. This one is called 'Repulsing the Monkey'." She finished the posture and joined Silas at the kitchen table where he had sat down with the newspaper. "Did I ever tell you about my penance from the priest at confession?" Silas shook his head, put down his newspaper, and she told him how annoyed she had been to be told she had to try harder.

"But I've been thinking about it since the day I took the twenty-question quiz. What would my life look like if I took Father's advice and tried harder?" Silas put his newspaper down and waited for her to go on. "Once I allowed myself to consider it, I knew it meant I should stop drinking. Our life is good, Silas, but something was missing. It's as though I have this potential I won't develop if I don't quit." He nodded, still silent. Maggie had the feeling he heard her, but didn't really understand her. She watched his attention revert to the sports page.

CHAPTER 8

"The thing I hate about office Christmas parties is looking for a job the next day." — Phyllis Diller

One bright sunny morning, Maggie walked into the side door of an old, white church, pulling the stubborn door forcibly to make it open. She walked past the children's nursery with its second-hand toys neatly stored in various colourful plastic tubs, past the washrooms and into a room painted light yellow with tables and chairs set in a large rectangle. People chatted near the coffee pot, some in their seats already, a few flipped through what looked like a small Bible. Posters adorned the walls with sayings like "Take it easy" and "Let go and let God." Maggie took off her coat and set it on the back of her chair. She had brought her own coffee from home, finding the coffee at AA too weak for her liking. Besides, all they had was the powdered cream substitute. If she went to the trouble of going to the gym and trying to eat properly and to stay sober, no way was she plugging her insides with that white death.

An elderly man beside her wore a baseball hat that said "Git 'er done" on the front; Maggie liked that saying.

Looking around the room, she saw people of all sorts in the chairs; they wore suits or tattered jeans, seemed hard-ridden or calm. Alcoholism is a great equalizer, she thought. What we all have in common is shame and guilt; booze has taken us on a one-way ride, but as one member once put it, "We don't have to ride the garbage truck all the way to the dump." Maggie shared with the others how it had been inconceivable to her, even a few months ago, that she could forego liquor. She figured that if she had fun when she was a child without alcohol, she could do so again.

In the late afternoon, Wendy invited Maggie over for a visit while her children were napping. She offered her a glass of wine, and although she didn't have to, Maggie decided to tell Wendy about her decision to quit drinking.

"Wow, I'm stunned," Wendy exclaimed, putting the kettle on for tea, instead. "Now, I wouldn't have pegged you as an alcoholic. You only ever have a couple of glasses of wine." She settled into the couch, taking a quick peek at George, asleep in his bassinet nearby.

"It's not how much you drink, it's how often and why." Maggie sighed. "I like it too much. I need it too much and it's compromised my relationships over the years in a subtle but damaging way. And it's a progressive disease."

"I guess being depressed didn't help?" Wendy said. Maggie nodded.

"I was able to function normally, at least on the outside, but I was so disconnected from my feelings I didn't recognize my anger as depression. I used alcohol to self-regulate, but it just made things worse; it made me more insular and irritated. By the way, thanks for putting me onto Lida Matthews; she's a doll."

Wendy couldn't believe Maggie actually attended AA meetings. "You don't fit the profile," she insisted, lifting a snuffling George gently from his bassinet.

"There is no profile." Maggie explained that the ideas of quitting drinking and attending AA didn't happen overnight, rather that things had built up to her making that decision — hangovers, living life in emotional chaos and spectacularly failing the Johns Hopkins test for alcoholism. "I had been looking at my obligations each day and trying to establish when I could fit in my glass of wine. For example, I pick up Harriet from swimming at nine in the evening; then, I'm home for the night, so I'm relieved that I can drink. That kind of pre-planning is classic alkie. It's called obsessive thinking in AA lingo."

"What about Christmas parties? Can you drink then?" Wendy asked, fixing George, now rooting vigorously, onto her right nipple. Maggie shook her head.

"Never again?"

Maggie nodded and Wendy shook her head in disbelief.

"That's why they say one day at a time." Maggie explained, getting up and making the tea. "Anything longer is incomprehensible. Actually, AA is very Zen, living in the moment and all that. "

"So how long do you have to attend AA?" Wendy asked.

"It's up to me, but I may do it for the rest of my life."

"Why? Once you're sober you're fine, right?"

"Wrong. AA believes that you're never cured. If I start again, even if it's 20 years from now, my body will react as though I never quit. There is no reward for time off; the disease remains strong even when I'm sober. I can't rely on myself alone to achieve sobriety and certainly not on friends. No offence, but friends justify my drinking and allow me to perpetuate it. I need to hear the harsh truth often by attending AA. I long ago missed the boat for casual drinking. Strangely enough, the idea behind AA is that it takes one alcoholic to help another maintain sobriety."

Maggie burped George while Wendy fixed her bra and sipped her tea. The conversation turned to whether Harriet might consider doing some babysitting for Wendy.

"I'll ask her." Maggie cuddled the baby some more and changed his diaper while Wendy helped her older child, Emma, now awake, to the potty.

CHAPTER 9

"On Christmas Eve my father would have 182 beers and then put our bikes together. 'Oh look, there are handlebars on my stereo. Why don't you have another highball and put some brakes on the dining room table with all those bolts you have left over?" — Kathleen Madigan

December rolled on through, a hurricane of shopping, wrapping and Christmas parties. Maggie's leg felt better; she still wore a tensor bandage, but it was healing. When Harriet got home from school, Maggie asked her whether she was interested in babysitting Wendy's two children occasionally. "It's a good way to earn a little pocket money," she said, encouragingly.

Harriet made a face. "I don't know. I'm not much of a kid person, Mom."

Maggie asked her how she would prefer to earn money. Harriet said she'd rather get a job in a restaurant or movie theatre. "I hear you get to see some movies for free when it's not busy!" she added excitedly.

So Maggie took Harriet to the movie theatre where she filled out an application form for employment. Shortly afterward, she had her first job interview and found herself with a schedule of work for weekend evenings.

On Christmas Eve, Beryl attended the evening mass with their family. Afterwards, they sang Christmas carols by the tree. Silas made eggnog from scratch (rum-free for Harriet and Maggie) and Beryl put some of her delicious butter tarts on a decorative plate. As the night wore on, Beryl went home and Harriet retired upstairs to allow the Santa Claus she no longer believed in to place gifts under the tree.

Maggie and Silas sat quietly by the glow of the Christmas tree, admiring its small white lights. These lights were a compromise for Maggie; she had always preferred the coloured lights. To her way of thinking, if you couldn't be a little tacky — even kitschy — at Christmas, then when could you? Marriages were made of compromise.

As they watched the fire flicker in the fireplace, Silas said, "I have a gift I'd like to give you tonight, Maggie."

"Don't you want Harriet to see me open it?"

"It's not wrapped," he said cryptically. Maggie smiled at him. Lately, she'd been conscious of being kinder to him, of trying to give him the benefit of the doubt. Yes, she had been angry at him for working too hard, for leaving much of the parenting to her, for procrastinating on things that were important to her and Harriet. But, as Lida had helped her to understand, these things have to be worked on together and over time. Maggie looked at him expectantly.

"My most important gift to you this Christmas is that I agree to go with you to see a marriage counsellor." As Maggie's eyes lit up, he added, "I have actually booked an appointment with Lida Matthews for the first Tuesday of January."

Maggie's eyes teared up with joy. She lunged at Silas, giving him a tight hug. "Oh thank you, Silas! This means so much to me!"

He patted her back gently and they lay dozing together on the sofa, firelight dancing on the walls, until the wee hours.

Harriet was the first awake on Christmas morning, not as early as she used to get up, but before her parents. She ransacked the contents of her stocking and then went back to bed for another hour. When Maggie got up to make coffee, the morning sky was just beginning to lighten. She enjoyed a hot cup by the twinkling lights of the Christmas tree as she waited for the other two to come downstairs.

All the gifts had been opened: electronics for Harriet and Silas, pyjamas and gift certificates all around. As Maggie gathered up tissue paper and bows for recycling, Harriet thrust a small box into her hands. "Here, Mom! Open this! It's from me and Dad." She stood impatiently by, waiting for Maggie to open it.

Maggie carefully removed the tape and wrapping on a ring box. Oh, she thought, Silas got me a new diamond ring. Maggie had noticed that the old setting was no longer where she had left it in the kitchen cupboard, so he probably took it and had a new diamond set into it. She wasn't totally surprised, but knew she must seem so for Harriet's sake. Opening the blue velvet box revealed instead a thick gold band, much wider than the one she'd had before, inlaid with a large oblong pink pearl. It reflected the light warmly; her eyes lit up.

"Is that the pearl...?" Maggie began.

"It's the pearl I got from Prudence! Remember, I showed it to you before? Doesn't it look beautiful, now?" Harriet grabbed the box from Maggie's hand and took the ring from it. Taking Maggie's left hand, she gently pushed the ring onto her fourth finger. It fit perfectly.

Maggie glanced at Silas, who smiled softly.

"I absolutely love it!" she exclaimed, holding her hand out to admire it. "Thank you, so much!" Tears rolled down her cheeks, dotting the front of her housecoat. Silas and Harriet came over and hugged her. Harriet let go of Maggie and bent down to pick up a piece of beige paper, darkened around the edges to look as though it were very old, rolled and tied with red velvet ribbon. Harriet unfurled the tiny scroll and read aloud:

The ancient history of this beautiful gem, the pearl, is as follows: In an attempt to convince Marc Anthony that

Egypt possessed a heritage and wealth that put it above conquest, Cleopatra wagered Marc Anthony that she could serve the most expensive dinner in history. He reclined as she sat with an empty plate and a goblet of wine. She crushed one large pair of pearl earrings, dissolved it in the wine and then drank it down. Astonished, Marc Anthony declined his dinner, the matching pearl, admitting that Cleopatra had won the wager.

Harriet looked eagerly to her parents for their reaction. They wiped joyful tears from their eyes and reached to Harriet for hugs. They held on for a moment, cuddling. Then Maggie suggested breakfast, so they all went to the kitchen for cinnamon buns and fruit.

Kristin Kraus

CHAPTER 10

"Once you become a pickle, you can't go back to being a cucumber." — Anonymous saying from AA

New Year's Day was cool and clear, a fresh start for Maggie. Looking over her calendar, she could see the dates where Harriet returned to school, an appointment for marriage counselling and a last physiotherapy appointment for her leg. She phoned the church to arrange for Harriet's confirmation in the spring, and then she sat at the computer to compose her resume. Typing in her contact information, she stopped and stared at the computer screen. It's hard to make your resume look impressive when you've been out of the work force for fourteen years. There's a huge gap, and anyway, why doesn't any of the volunteer work you've done at your child's school count for much in the world of paid work? She began the resume with her computer course, describing it as though already completed. She decided that she'd have to do some current volunteering in her field to flesh out the resume. Feeling a bit better, she saved her file and left the house to meet Wendy and her babies for a short walk.

As Wendy pushed her double stroller full of cherubic little people, she asked how Maggie's sobriety was coming along.

"My fridge is full of every possible juice and soda you can think of," Maggie said, smiling. "And I don't even like those much, so I have to dilute them with sparkling water. It's all very complicated. And I've been avoiding the pub. I still see my pub buddies, but I see them at yoga or the coffee shop instead of the bar." Wendy wanted to know if her pub buddies treated her any differently now that she was off the sauce, but Maggie didn't think so.

"If anything, they're curious about my sobriety. I probably do miss out on some social invites involving the pub, but that's a small price to pay in the big scheme of things. I have to think of myself, my family and my mental health."

"Do you miss it — the beer, the wine?" Wendy asked.

"Hell, yes! But it's a temporary thought and the feeling passes quickly. I miss liquor the way you miss an old boyfriend who was never any good for you anyway. I miss getting drunk for what I think it should be, not for what it really is for me."

"Do you get delirium tremens?" Wendy asked quietly, glancing at her children as if worried they might be listening. Maggie shook her head.

"No, thank God. I'm getting out in time, getting off the crazy train. Some people at AA talk about detox though, and it sounds horrific, like something you wouldn't sic on your worst enemy." Wendy wondered aloud if the AA meetings were a drag.

"Actually, I enjoy them. I look forward to them." Maggie answered. "People share their experiences — if they want to, that is. Some people are doing really well and have years of sobriety under their belts, but some people are right out of treatment and struggling. We all have our disease in common."

"Disease?" Wendy asked sceptically.

"The founder of AA was a doctor. He believed that people who are alcoholic have a different reaction to alcohol than other people; he compares it to an allergy. You and I can both drink, but it will affect me more, and I will, over time, begin to obsess about it. Over the years, alcohol started to dominate my thoughts and dictate daily decisions. For example, I'd choose one restaurant over another, not because I liked the food, but because I could walk home from it. Or I'd organize my evening carpool so I could drink sooner." She paused and looked down. "Relationships suffer for it, too. Booze, for the alcoholic, has an insidious effect."

Wendy remained quiet, thoughtful. "You've given me a lot to think about," she said.

With Harriet's confirmation coming up, Maggie offered to buy her a new dress. Harriet tried on her dress shoes and found that they still fit. The stores already had their winter clothes on sale and the spring collection hung cheerfully in the window displays. Maggie followed Harriet around the store as she picked several dresses off the racks and took them to the fitting room.

"Come out and show me the dresses when you have them on." Maggie called over the fitting room door.

"This one's brutal. I'm not showing you." Harriet made rustling sounds in there as she hastily removed the rejected garment, which she unceremoniously flung over the top of the door. She carried on that way until she found just the right dress. Harriet stepped grandly out of the fitting room in a light green creation, sleeves slightly puffed with silky fabric flowing to just above her knees.

"It's like it was made for you!" Maggie exclaimed. She took the dress to the cashier to pay for it while Harriet put her own clothes back on. As they left the store, Harriet convinced her mother that the dress shoes she had tried on at home were not well-suited to this new dress, and Maggie agreed to buy her a new pair.

"Hey, Hanky, how would you like to put your fashion sense to work and help me buy some new outfits? I need a makeover." Harriet's eyes lit up, "Sure thing, Mom!" Off they went to choose a few items for Maggie, too.

Once back home, Maggie made herself a cup of organic loose leaf tea (expensive tea being a gift to herself since she quit drinking) and wrote in her journal.

I should feel proud of myself, instead, I feel rebellious against my alcoholism. Why am I an alcoholic? I never signed up for this. Actually, I did,

I just didn't realize it at the time. How fair is that? This rebelliousness translates into a current resentment of AA. Logically, I know I need to attend meetings so I don't start to think I can go back to drinking, but childishly, I am pushing against its demands. Lida told me I should get an AA sponsor soon, someone you get together with outside of meetings and phone when your resolve is weak. I've been keeping an eye out at meetings for someone I could ask, but the whole idea doesn't appeal to me. I'm also supposed to join an AA Big Book study group (that's like the Bible for AA). Sounds about as much fun as paper cuts between the toes. I've never been interested in studying the actual Bible that way and this sounds even less interesting to me. I do own the Big Book, got it at a meeting, and I've read bits and pieces of it here and there. The thought of reading it cover to cover scares me. It's overwhelming. The idea of sitting with a group of near-strangers and parsing its text leaves me cold.

I know I'm being pig-headed (apparently that's common among alcoholics). Our egos are partly to blame for our drinking problems and our stubbornness keeps us there longer than is good for us. I know that I should strive to meet people at AA and allow them to help me; truly, there is no greater unconditional acceptance than you will find at an AA meeting, but still I balk. I continue to go to meetings, but I keep a distance. The meeting facilitator gave me heck last time (gently) for not phoning her. She was just trying to reach out to me, but I need more time. They gave me a list of

> *women from AA that I can phone anytime I need to, but I don't want to. I've spent a good part of my life being independent and I don't want to change.*
>
> *Maybe it's because of the way I came into AA, when times were relatively good and of my own volition. The unmanageability of my life happened mostly in the past; now I'm doing a pre-emptive strike against alcoholism's worst. By contrast, some people from AA have come to the meeting after climbing out of a garbage bin. They have lost everything important to them so they are grateful to AA for providing support, boundaries and security. For me though, meetings are taking up time I used to go to tai chi, or do housework or whatever. I had a life before AA and I want it back.*

At Richmond University, Maggie parked her car in the pay lot. She had left the house in good time in case she got lost on campus. It had been several years since she'd been there and there were new unfamiliar buildings. Would she be the oldest in her class, a forty-something among twenty-somethings? She found her class easily and had time to buy a cup of coffee. Awkwardly, she realized that she couldn't have her drink near the keyboards of the computers, so she put it on the floor under her chair and shortly afterward, accidentally kicked it over. Scrambling around in her purse, she found enough napkins to clean it up. As she did so, she realized that only a mother would have napkins in her purse. She felt old.

When the morning came for Silas and Maggie's first appointment with Lida Matthews, they entered the reception area gingerly. Maggie hung her coat up and Silas followed suit, wiping his hands nervously on his pants.

"It's okay, she doesn't bite," Maggie reassured him. They thumbed through dated magazines until it was their turn.

At the Chesapeake Bay Hatchery Maggie rang the silver bell on the counter for service. Prudence came out front, chewing as if her lunch had just been interrupted. "Hello, may I help you?" she asked.

"Hi, I'm Maggie McCaffrey. I was wondering if you needed any volunteers here."

Prudence smiled, revealing a large gap between her front teeth. "You look familiar."

"My daughter is involved with the oyster project." Prudence nodded and said, "We're always happy to see volunteers. What's your background?"

"I have a bachelor's degree in science." They negotiated some flexible times when Maggie could come and log into the computer information about oyster rehabilitation projects. Prudence offered Maggie a cup of herbal tea and gave her a tour of the facility.

Over a cup of tea, Maggie told Wendy, "I got my 60-day chip last week." The coffee shop had a playroom for Emily; George, as usual, slept in his stroller. At Wendy's quizzical look, Maggie explained the AA system of rewards. "They give you a chip marker, a coin of sorts, for milestones in sobriety. So I received the 7 day, 14, 21, 30, and now 60 days. The next chip is for 90 days of sobriety, and then one year."

"And that really motivates you?" Wendy asked.

"Strangely, enough, yes. I mean, you go up and receive it and everybody claps for you. It's like being in school again without the judgment. Then people come up to you after and congratulate you. It's hard not to like that."

"Weird."

"Well, I do feel a bit funny about it at times. Like now, I'm going to have to wait three months before I see another chip. That's a long time for me to go without external reinforcement!"

"I used to have an uncle who was alcoholic," Wendy said. "He used to tell us when he was planning on a binge; he called it 'going on tour' or 'his tour of duty,' like he was an army guy or something." She added sugar to her latte and gave it a vigorous stir.

Maggie laughed. "We used to say in college that we were going to get 'absolutely Moulin-rouged'."

Now Wendy laughed, almost choking on her drink. "There sure are a lot of jokey words for being drunk and puking."

Maggie reeled off as many as she could think of, "the gastro geyser, jettisoning the chunky cargo, reviewing today's menu…" She stopped talking to catch her breath, they were laughing so hard.

Wendy's shoulders shook. "How about my all-time favourite: riding the regurgitron." This started more crazed hilarity, which ended with Maggie spilling her tea. When the two finally calmed down, Maggie returned to the table with napkins. Wendy asked her why she thought there were so many euphemisms.

"I think the slang normalizes the experience," Maggie said, becoming more serious. "If we commiserate with friends over a bad hangover, we can minimize the seriousness of our drinking problems, deny them, in fact, and the shame that goes with them."

"But, doesn't everyone overdo it sometimes?" Wendy asked.

"I don't know, Wendy. Maybe because I'm an alcoholic, I just know a lot of other alcoholics. Is it normal to make yourself barf from liquor? To wake up and you don't know how you got where you are? To get the gambles?"

"The what?"

"You haven't heard that one? It's when you drink too much beer and the next day you are afraid to fart in case it's not just air."

Wendy guffawed, then said, "It's sad that there's a word for that."

"And that I know it." Maggie shook her head ruefully.

At home, Harriet was looking in the kitchen drawer for a pad of sticky notes. She picked up a round coin that read 60 days on one side and had something called the Serenity Prayer on the other. Remembering what she had read in her mother's journal, she realized that this must be from AA. She put it back where she had found it and closed the drawer, feeling a twinge of guilt for reading her mother's private thoughts. Harriet thought of homeless people, lecherous great uncles and the like when she thought of drinkers, but her mother? And yet she wrote of it in her journal so frequently.

CHAPTER 11

Carl Jung referred to alcoholics as frustrated mystics, believing them to actually be searching for spiritual enlightenment, but going about it the wrong way.

Three weeks after completing her computer course, Maggie's marks arrived in the mail. She proudly showed Harriet her "report card." Harriet, at that point, was preparing the data sheets for her oyster garden. The time had come to count the live and dead and fill out the final forms. She would keep the oysters until late spring, when the hatchery would introduce them into the bay population.

Maggie's resume was taking shape: her actual course mark, her volunteer work at the hatchery and a few recent references (Prudence and her professor). She decided to include a brief summary of her job of years ago at the department of environmental quality and went on to do some research for jobs.

The evening of her confirmation Harriet came home from school and showered, spending an eternity in the bathroom curling her long blond hair and dressing for the event. While Silas also dressed, Maggie prepared a vegetable platter and dip for the celebration after the ceremony. She was thankful that Beryl and Wendy could make it. Wendy was becoming a very good friend, and it meant a lot to Maggie that she was attending the confirmation. She wasn't even a relative, not obligated in any way. The sandwiches she had fixed earlier were taking up a lot of room in the fridge, so Maggie moved them to the downstairs fridge. They used to keep that fridge full of beer, but with Maggie not drinking anymore, there was actually room in it for food. Didn't everyone have a beer fridge? Maggie thought wryly.

Earlier that day, she had baked a chocolate cake (Harriet's favourite) and used a store-bought blue gel icing to create a crucifix in the centre of its rectangular surface. With her hand as steady as she could make it, she wrote "Congratulations, Harriet!" in cursive script. Stepping back, she acknowledged that no one would mistake it for a professional pastry chef's work, but that it was passable. Maggie remembered how hard she used to be on herself. In the past, she would be crying right now because she had not been able to make the lettering perfect.

Harriet looked radiant in her pretty green dress, wearing a silver crucifix around her neck, one that Silas had bought for her. Although not overly religious, Maggie felt proud of her daughter and thankful for this sense of occasion, a ritual of passage in a society that doesn't have many anymore.

Today's AA meeting topic was "Maintaining Sobriety." I decided to share when called upon, expressing the idea that the word "sobriety" itself has a negative connotation in our society. We think of expressions like "sober as a judge," not anything anyone envies or aspires to. Author Kingsley Amis, one of many literary alcoholics, noted the peculiar connection of alcohol to hilarity. Think of all the times you laughed with your friends over beers, things that were funny seemed more so with liquor. Before quitting, I worried that I'd lose my sense of humour. If I didn't drink, I wouldn't be any fun to be around anymore. It's an irrational fear, but it keeps many alcoholics drinking. We tend to have low self-esteem and our belief in our talents and our sense of humour is weak. I joked that we should hire a publicist to rename and rebrand the concept of sobriety.

In Lida's office, Maggie recounted her AA sharing and her reluctance to embrace the idea of having a sponsor; the novelty of quitting was definitely wearing off now that she'd been sober for about four months. Lida encouraged her to keep going to meetings and to share those feelings because wisdom comes from those who have been there and conquered the same demons.

"It is part of the disease of alcoholism that the afflicted tell themselves that they are not really alcoholic and therefore do not need AA. If you lose touch with that support system, you may backslide," Lida warned. "You can't afford to forget how vulnerable you are to addiction."

This last statement reminded Maggie to tell Lida about her weight gain. "I think I'm getting addicted to dessert," she joked. "I've noticed all my pants are tighter. Either I'm gaining weight, or toxic elves have shrunk all my pants as they hang in my closet."

Lida laughed. Maggie admitted that she knew about the importance of exercise and healthy eating, and just needed to apply it more rigorously. A large slice of banana bread every afternoon did not need to become her new habit. She didn't want to trade one addiction for another, but it wasn't easy.

"When I'm at a social event, I feel like I'm entitled to lots of dessert because I'm not having liquor. I figure the calories I would have had from the alcohol have just switched to the cake so, it's okay."

"Lots of alcoholics gain weight when they quit," Lida said, "because they didn't used to eat properly when they were drinking. Booze took the place of food. Just watch so your weight doesn't creep up too much." She recommended that Maggie try different AA meetings. Maggie told her that she had attended one that was for women only and that she was surprised to see seventy-year-olds there.

"Will I still be going to AA in my twilight years?" Maggie wondered aloud.

Lida was not surprised. "Maybe. People make friends there and keep going to the meetings partly because of the social aspect. Also, there is no cure for alcoholism. One day at a time means just that — forever. It beats the alternative, though."

"I don't want to believe I'm incurable, that I'll wear this badge of shame until the day I kick the bucket. I hate that you don't ever "graduate" from AA; it's like the friggin' Hotel California — you can check out any time you like, but you can never leave!" Maggie shuddered.

Lida smiled at that. "Any other beefs with AA?"

"Now that you mention it, yes! I hate it when someone is on their way to the bathroom and says that they've had too much coffee. Who cares? I don't want to think about the composition or output of your urine! If you have to go, go. Don't justify the frequency or duration of your trips. Just go."

"Nice rant," Lida joked. "Anything else?"

"Yeah, the coffee there. I know it's made and poured by volunteers, but go ahead and put another spoonful of grounds in that filter!"

"You could bring your own coffee," Lida suggested.

Maggie nodded. "I do. I've given up liquor, so I need a strong good cup of joe." She paused and added, "I think that's all I've got."

Lida laughed and Maggie felt better.

Maggie went over to Wendy's on a sunny June afternoon to look after the two children for a few hours while Wendy did some shopping. Harriet stopped her just as she was leaving the house, and asked if she could come with her.

As Maggie locked their front door, she tried to be casual and asked Harriet whatever had become of Jackson, the party boy.

"Oh, I dumped him. He's an ass." Ignoring the profanity, in fact, mentally agreeing with it, Maggie asked what happened.

"Well, you know he likes to get drunk, and since I've been working a lot at the theatre, I don't have time for him. He's a loser, anyway." Harriet pretended to be looking intently at something on her sweater.

"There are nicer boys out there for you, Harriet." Maggie said as they strolled over to Wendy's. She put her arm around her daughter's shoulder, pleased that Harriet didn't shrug her off.

"Yeah, I can do better." Harriet smiled. "Anyway, there's this guy, Joseph, who works at the theatre, too. He's pretty nice to me."

Maggie's cell phone rang; it was someone named Burt from the nearby city of Woodbridge. He had read her resume and was interested in seeing her for a job interview for an environmental quality enforcement compliance specialist. She would conduct compliance inspections, review plant records and evaluate technical reports. Maggie hung up and phoned Silas right away.

"How's Hanky going to feel about you working?" he asked.

Maggie sighed and wondered why there is always so much guilt for mothers. "I'd like to give the job a try, Silas. If it really doesn't work out, I'm not tied to it for life." She could imagine him nodding slowly on the other end of the line.

At the hatchery, Maggie and Harriet returned their oysters. Prudence asked them if they would take on new spat in August. Harriet looked at Maggie for approval and she agreed. Returning to the car, Maggie said, "I didn't mind looking after those oysters, how about you?"

"Yeah, I liked that project." Harriet answered. "And since we already have all the cages and hoses, why not?"

Dusk was falling as Harriet set up her new oyster spat on the dock. Her parents sipped tea by the outdoor fireplace. Waves lapped rhythmically at the shore; fireflies blinked by and by, and the silence felt like emotional velvet. Maggie lifted up her left hand towards her husband.

"You know, Silas, this pearl means a lot to me, for a couple of reasons. Obviously because you and Harriet put it into a ring for me with that neat story about Cleopatra." Silas nodded, accepting the thanks. "It also because it reminds me of my depression."

Frowning, Silas set down his mug. "How's that a good thing?"

"Because I'm beating it. I've quit drinking, I'm taking care of myself and I'm getting help. I know I'm a depressive and an alcoholic, but that's not all I am and I refuse to let it wear me down. Depression is sneaky; it'll compromise everything if you let it. It seems to have a devious intelligence, like cancer. It knows better than to strike all at once. Instead, it spreads confusion and dismay slowly over decades, locking you down more effectively."

He looked at her quizzically and Maggie continued, "I'm like an oyster in a way, responding to irritants by creating nacre in thin concentric layers steadily over time."

"So what irritates an oyster?" Silas smiled.

"Could be a sharp object or parasite that the oyster can't expel."

"Like your mother?" Silas guffawed. Maggie smiled wryly. "This nacre is the result of my depression, my response to the crap life dishes out. This pearl is a sign of the hidden beauty of wisdom that is mine, if I beat depression and alcoholism."

"Wow, that's deep." Silas said, staring out at the water. "Any regrets?"

"I try not to regret. It's like guilt, a wasted emotion. I do owe an apology to Father though, for rejecting his confessional wisdom. I was so quick to discount what he said to me about having to try harder, when he was actually as astute as if he had seen right into my soul. That is a perfect example of alcoholic arrogance. Even though I wasn't drunk at the time of my confession, my unhealthy pride affected my ability to see how he might be right."

Harriet came out of the house and pulled up a chair nearby, her cheeks a healthy pink. "Hey, I just measured my new oysters. They've already grown one inch!"

Her parents smiled proudly at her and at each other. Maggie saw how Harriet was also like a pearl, a beautiful gift coming into this world through her and Silas. Like a pearl, Harriet was unique, lovely and maturing, despite (or perhaps because) of a sometimes hostile environment. Maggie knew that she was, at times, an irritant to Harriet. She prayed that her influence on her daughter be for the best, if not wholly positive all the time, at least benign. Let other people be the bad example, the ones who show her child how not to be. Months ago, Maggie would have been sitting on this deck downing her second or third glass of wine, blathering on meaninglessly about nothing of consequence, oblivious to the emotional needs of anyone, herself included. Now, no beer (import or domestic), no wine (table, house, sommelier-approved, even boxed), no rum and eggnog mixed to smooth, sweet perfection, no buzz, regardless of its temporary relief, was worth the steady leaching of this simple familial joy. Once an alcoholic, always an alcoholic? There are worse things to be.

The End